For my mom and dad, who always taught me to be accepting of everyone. Thank you for serving as a constant inspiration to my biggest dreams.

And for God, who always was there for me, even in the darkest times.

Kindness Is Key

Alexis Bloomer

Copyright © 2017 Alexis Bloomer.

All rights reserved. No part of this book may be used or reproduced by any means, graphic, electronic, or mechanical, including photocopying, recording, taping or by any information storage retrieval system without the written permission of the author except in the case of brief quotations embodied in critical articles and reviews.

This book is a work of non-fiction. Unless otherwise noted, the author and the publisher make no explicit guarantees as to the accuracy of the information contained in this book and in some cases, names of people and places have been altered to protect their privacy.

Archway Publishing books may be ordered through booksellers or by contacting:

Archway Publishing
1663 Liberty Drive
Bloomington, IN 47403
www.archwaypublishing.com
1 (888) 242-5904

Because of the dynamic nature of the Internet, any web addresses or links contained in this book may have changed since publication and may no longer be valid. The views expressed in this work are solely those of the author and do not necessarily reflect the views of the publisher, and the publisher hereby disclaims any responsibility for them.

Any people depicted in stock imagery provided by Thinkstock are models, and such images are being used for illustrative purposes only.
Certain stock imagery © Thinkstock.

ISBN: 978-1-4808-4793-4 (sc)
ISBN: 978-1-4808-4794-1 (hc)
ISBN: 978-1-4808-4792-7 (e)

Print information available on the last page.

Archway Publishing rev. date: 8/17/2017

Some girls wear pink with bows and such,
while other girls think that's a little much.

Some boys love basketball, baseball, and more,
while other little boys would rather study than explore.

There are one hundred ways to be,
but there is only one you. That's incredible; you'll see!

Our world is as big as you and me,
so it's important to remember-kindness is always key.

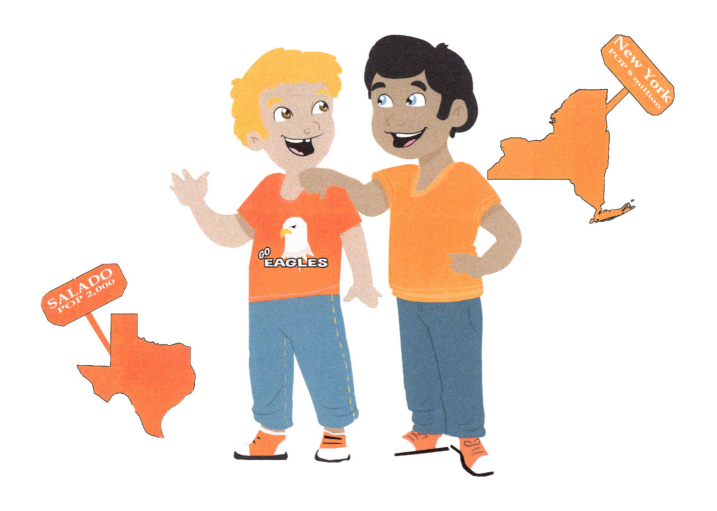

Kids come from all over the world.
From big cities with tall buildings and bright lights
To small towns where they do not even have stoplights.

Little ones come from everywhere; each is equally rare.
So to judge even one would simply be unfair!

You smile, you laugh, you yell, and you cry.
You say hi, and you even say goodbye!

You're more alike than you see, so kindness is always key!

No matter where you're from or the color of your skin, everyone deserves to fit in.

No matter their color, don't judge right away because the words that you say are always there to stay.

No matter what you look like, what you do or what you say, choose kindness and you'll lead the way.

No one is able to make you change when you're proud of who you are and don't think it's strange.

Always remember: you're great, no matter your height or weight!

Be kind and the world will love you too; just wait.

Unfortunately, not all will choose
kindness or agree with your views.

Some kids will not be able to relate,
so instead they will turn to hate
and try to make you the bully bait.

But *no!* That is not your fate;
you won't give in and make that mistake.

You are strong and impossible to break,
and that will always be hard for the bully to take.

It might seem easier to cry or give up,
but don't let the bullies win—
they are defenseless if you don't let them in.

You'll notice this happens to all;
even the greatest of kids sometimes fall—
but never for long because they know it is wrong.

No matter your background, don't join along—
all people should feel like they belong.

A bully doesn't pick and choose;
even the cool kids can experience the bully blues!

The girl with all the friends gets teased about what she wears, and even the star athlete gets teased because his parents aren't millionaires.

As you can see, everyone has a battle. The little boy who wears boots gets made fun of for being country.

And sometimes you're not from America at all and people make fun of your drawl. You get left out because you don't know what being "country" is all about.

No one gets left out when it comes to being bully bait; that's why it's always better to tell someone rather than wait.

If you see someone being mean to a kid,
help the kid out and don't just flee—
always let an adult intervene.

No one wants to feel unloved, even if he or she is
different—that is something to be proud of.

But sometimes it's not like that at all;
see, bullies can come from every which way,
and they sometimes even do it when the adults are away.

When you're alone, it's easier for the bully to not get caught—and every coward likes this thought.

Bullies are not always bright; they should know
that strong kids never go down without a fight.
Don't fist fight, but instead just do what's right.

You see, you're never alone,
and it's up to you to tell someone who is grown.

That doesn't make you a tattletale; it makes you a hero,
and it ensures that the bullying days are limited to zero.

As you grow up, it might be hard to blend in,
but if you stay kind, you'll always win.

So keep your chin up, and don't let them get under
your skin—most important, don't let the bully in.

I was once in your shoes and experienced the bullying blues. It made me strong, and I learned that bullying is always wrong. Like you, I tried to be friends with all—even those who made me feel small.

And from the girl who is different than most, I'm telling you to stay strong—because you're getting so close!

When you choose kindness,
you'll be different from the rest,
and you'll realize that being nice
is always best.

Everyone has something that makes him or her unique,
so kindness is what we all should seek.

Kindness is key, and we all know
that is something we'll never outgrow.

Kindness Pact:

Sign below if you will practice kindness daily.

_____

Name three friends who practice kindness every day:

1. _____

2. _____

3. _____

How can you be more kind?

_____

In *Kindness Is Key*, your child will learn to *associate kindness with rhyming*. This story was created to teach young children the importance of knowing what a bully is and also how to do the right thing if they see bullying taking place around them. Growing up, I was a victim of bullying, and I believe that we have to start teaching children from a young age to not judge each other. Instead, we should teach our children to accept that everyone is different. This book was created to promote self-love and to teach children to appreciate one another's differences. I hope that with my book, *Kindness Is Key*, your child will remember these rhymes and apply them to everyday life. Together, we can prove that *kindness still matters*.

CPSIA information can be obtained
at www.ICGtesting.com
Printed in the USA
BVHW02s1734120918
527313BV00009B/31/P